Surrounded by Grace

A Bible Study for Lent

Bill Thomas

CSS Publishing Company, Inc.
Lima, Ohio

SURROUNDED BY GRACE

FIRST EDITION
Copyright © 2017
by CSS Publishing Co., Inc.

Library of Congress Cataloging-in-Publication Data
Names: Thomas, Bill, 1965- author.
Title: Surrounded by grace : Lenten Bible study / Bill Thomas.
Description: FIRST EDITION. | Lima, Ohio : CSS Publishing Company, Inc., 2017.
Identifiers: LCCN 2017010580| ISBN 9780788028830 (pbk. : alk. paper) | ISBN 0788028839 (pbk.) Subjects: LCSH: Lent--Textbooks.
Classification: LCC BV85 .T453 2017 | DDC 242/.34--dc23
LC record available at https://lccn.loc.gov/2017010580

For more information about CSS Publishing Company resources, visit our website at www.csspub.com, email us at csr@csspub.com, or call (800) 241-4056.

Cover photo © michaelshake / 123RF Stock Photo. (https://www.123rf.com/profile_michaelshake)

e-book:
ISBN-13: 978-0-7880-2884-7
ISBN-10: 0-7880-2884-7

ISBN-13: 978-0-7880-2883-0
ISBN-10: 0-7880-2883-9   PRINTED IN USA

To Sean and Kimber Gilbert:
May you always be surrounded by his grace.

Table of Contents

Acknowledgments   7
Introduction   9
How to Use this Book   11

Lesson 1   13
Grace for Those Awkward Moments

Lesson 2   23
Grace to Overcome What Was

Lesson 3   35
Grace for the Times When Life's Too Hard

Lesson 4   45
Grace for the Broken Heart

Lesson 5   55
Grace When Things Are Chaotic

Lesson 6   65
Grace on Display

Lesson 7   75
Grace Delivered

Acknowledgments

I want to thank the following people for their help in getting this book ready.

David Runk and his staff at CSS Publishing Company for allowing me the opportunity to write about our Lord and Savior Jesus Christ.

Dave Smith and Dottie Bodewitz, coworkers at First Christian Church in Washington, for reading early drafts, offering suggestions and proofreading.

Nichole Ridner for her encouragement and her skills in proofreading.

My parents, Bill and Joyce Thomas, for all their support.

My Lord and Savior Jesus Christ about whom and for whom it is written.

Introduction

"Come out with your hands up. We've got you surrounded!"

If you're a fan of old westerns or cops and robbers shows, you've no doubt heard that expression. It's usually the conclusion of a climactic fight at which point the good guys are closing in on the bad guys, leaving them no option but surrender. In simpler times, this was the point at which we'd cheer that virtue triumphs over evil.

Today, though, I think that old line applies in a different way. No matter what direction we turn, it seems we find problems. Whether it's financial uncertainty, world and national security, health issues, trouble with parents or tension with kids, we are surrounded by difficulties, demanding that we "come out with our hands up."

Is there anything we can do? Is there any hope? As we enter Lent and approach Easter, I think there's something else out there, too. The challenging situations we deal with are still around, threatening and making unreasonable demands. However, something else surrounds us, too. A walk through John's gospel reminds us that where problems abound, grace abounds even more. I hope this study leading into Easter will help you realize that when the "bad guys" of this life are closing in, taunting you saying, "All is lost," you can be strengthened by his grace.

How to Use this Book

The studies contained in this book can be used in different ways. First, they can be utilized as an individual study in which the participant reads the material and interacts with it as the lesson directs. The book is also designed to be used in a small group setting. In that manner, the leader of the group should study the lesson in advance, noting the objective for each lesson and the accompanying prayer focus. The lesson can be read in the group and, if desired, appropriate songs can be selected from the list. There are some questions found at the end of each lesson that can be used to spark discussion.

The material in this book also may be used as sermon material throughout the Lenten season. Each lesson could be used as a springboard into a sermon. Appropriate illustrations and applications are included in each one. The lessons might also be part of a combined worship/study experience. A speaker could read part of the lesson in a worship setting. Appropriate songs could be sung. Discussion of the text and questions might then follow. However this study is used, it is my prayer that it will remind you of the amazing grace of our Lord and Savior.

Lesson 1

Grace for Those Awkward Moments

Lesson Objective: At the end of this lesson, each participant will understand that Jesus Christ cares about the simple or little things of life and has the power and ability to change, even the smallest things, for our benefit.

Prayer Focus: Pray that each one involved in this lesson would see the incredible love and presence of Jesus at work in the awkward or embarrassing situations of life.

Scripture Reference: John 2:1-11
On the third day there was a wedding in Cana of Galilee, and the mother of Jesus was there. Jesus and his disciples had also been invited to the wedding. When the wine gave out, the mother of Jesus said to him, "They have no wine." And Jesus said to her, "Woman, what concern is that to you and to me? My hour has not yet come." His mother said to the servants, "Do whatever he tells you." Now standing there were six stone water jars for the Jewish rites of purification, each holding twenty or thirty gallons. Jesus said to them, "Fill the jars with water." And they filled them up to the brim. He said to them, "Now draw some out, and take it to the chief steward." So they took it. When the steward tasted the water that had become wine, and did not know where it came from (though the servants who had drawn the water knew), the steward called the bridegroom and said to him,

"Everyone serves the good wine first, and then the inferior wine after the guests have become drunk. But you have kept the good wine until now." Jesus did this, the first of his signs, in Cana of Galilee, and revealed his glory; and his disciples believed in him.

Awkward Moments

Have you ever felt out of place and that all eyes were looking at you? Have you ever done or said something that you knew, right away, was the wrong thing to say or do? Though we try to avoid them, those awkward moments happen.

The scholarship tea was to be held at the alumni association's ballroom and I was thrilled to get an invitation. I'd been chosen to receive a scholarship. It wasn't a large one, but it was a scholarship nonetheless. I was excited and happy to go. At this point, I need to tell you that I had not been to very many fancy engagements and I'd never been to the alumni association building for any reason at all. I wasn't sure how to dress for such an event. I knew it required more than jeans and a t-shirt. I'd been to a few other awards events and knew that the dress was business casual. So, I put on slacks, a collared shirt and a sweater and went. I realized not long after I'd arrived that I'd made a mistake. Nearly everyone was in a suit and tie. No one said anything and I still got the award, but I remember how I felt.

I'm sure you've experienced some of those awkward moments, too. The times that you wish you could stop and rewind things to do it over again, only better. Sometimes they are embarrassing incidents that leave little or no lasting damage. They become the things that we look back on and laugh at how foolish or naïve we once were. However, there are some situations that leave painful scars. There are some that create a lifetime of regret and remorse.

It was only the push of a button and a quick glance at a website, but now the job is gone and with it a reputation.

It was only a few angry words; the heat of the moment, but they were heard, internalized and now the relationship will never be the same.

It was just one time. No one would see, but someone did and now a witness is compromised, and character is forever stained.

The supervisor was unfair and biased, but the job was gone, just the same.

What can we do when these situations are upon us? Is there any way we can make them go away? The key is found in God's grace. Grace; it is a remarkable, wonderful word that is hard to define, but even harder to live without. The traditional definition of grace is God's unmerited favor given to us. That definition works and makes sense theologically. However, to really understand grace, you have to experience it.

Do you want to know what grace is? Ask a former thief who hung next to Jesus at the place of the Skull. He can tell you.

Still searching for what grace is? Ask the prostitute turned protector. Her name is Rahab. You'll find her in the family tree of Jesus.

Grace is what gets us through those tough times of life. Grace is what reminds us that no matter how dark it is, the sun will rise. I know what you're thinking. "Sure, they know about grace. Look at them. They went from one extreme to the other. But what about me? I've never been too bad, but I know something's not right. I've got my problems. What can grace do for me?"

Today we look at a regular couple that was facing a real problem, at least for them. Jesus handles their problem in a way that describes what his grace can do for regular folks. Let's take a look.

As chapter 2 of John opens, Jesus and his disciples are invited to a wedding. Jesus' mother is also at this wedding. Before we get into the details of what happened, let's take a look at some relevant context.

The Wedding at Cana

Chronologically, the wedding at Cana takes place after Jesus encounters Nathanael, who declares him to be the Son of God, and likely three days after John baptizes him in the Jordan near Bethany. The trip to Cana from Bethany would've likely taken about two days. The wedding was on the third day. Cana is a village in the hills of Galilee. It is about nine miles north of Nazareth, where Jesus grew up, and may well be the present-day city of Khirbet Qana.

Weddings in Jesus' day were a bit different than in twenty-first century America. A wedding at that time was a gala occasion and, especially in a village like Cana, would be a community celebration that could last a week. Refreshments were provided by the couple for all of the guests, and of these refreshments, wine was very important. To fail in providing adequately for guests at a wedding was a huge social disgrace. In a small community like Cana, such an error would never be forgotten and would haunt the newly married couple the rest of their lives.

Why were Jesus, his disciples, and Mary at the wedding? First, let's note why they weren't there. They weren't there because they were celebrities. They weren't well-known, at least, not yet. They weren't there because Jesus was seen as a great spiritual leader and miracle worker. He wasn't, yet. They weren't there because their names could be dropped later; *Yes, well you know, we had Jesus at our wedding.. Yeah, uh huh.* Neither the bride nor the groom knew what Jesus was going to do. None of those are the reason. What is it, then? Simply this: they were invited. Verse 2 makes that clear. They were there because the bride and groom knew Jesus and wanted him to come. Maybe they were related somehow. Maybe they were just good friends who grew up together in Nazareth. The point is, though, Jesus was invited to come, so he went.

Beyond Awkward

As we read in verse 3, a problem arises to mar this happy occasion. They are out of wine. To our twenty-first century minds, this seems like a problem, but not a mortifying situation. However, as we've noted earlier, running out of wine in this culture would be a disgrace that would taint this couple's future for a long time. Jesus' mother is aware of the predicament and is direct in her words to him. "They have no wine." That's it. Pretty straightforward and clear. She knows what it means, and Jesus is aware of the connotations, too. This is a bad situation; a tight spot.

The Story of Jazz, the Puppy

A puppy named Jazz knew a bit about a tight spot. Firefighters were called to a family's home after their puppy got her head trapped in the metal garden gate. The 15-week-old Hungarian Vizsla, Jazz, was trapped for about an hour while family members, firefighters and numbers of neighbors tried everything they could think of to free her — including covering her in vegetable oil! When all else failed, the firefighters used the equipment they use to free humans from vehicle wreckages to set Jazz free.

How did Jazz end up stuck in the gate? Jazz had been enthusiastically running toward the front drive. Oblivious to where she was and what she was doing, she just dashed ahead. Failing to stop in time, she crashed into the gate and her head became lodged in one of the small holes in the side gate.

Can you imagine the scene? An out of control dog crashes into a fence and gets her head stuck between the bars. Since Jazz was unhurt and later freed, that's a humorous and pointed story. Life, with its unexpected circumstances, runs out of control sometimes. When it does, it creates all kinds of predicaments. It happened to Jazz. It happened to an unnamed bride and groom. It happens to all of us.

Jesus Acts in a Tight Spot

Mary mentions to Jesus, "They have no wine." What will Jesus do? He answers, "Woman, what concern is that to you and to me? My hour has not yet come." It sounds a bit strange to us, but it isn't what it appears to be on the surface. Jesus isn't being rude or disrespectful. The word "woman" in the Greek language carries with it a sense of respect and affection. It is the same word Jesus later uses on the cross when he says, "Woman, behold your son." He continues to say that this is not the time for him to declare that he is the Messiah that both he and she know he is. However, something else must've taken place, too. Something between the words in verse 4 and Mary's instructions to the servants in verse 5. Maybe it was a wink, maybe a nod or maybe just an unspoken assurance, but whatever it was, Mary got it and told the servants to do whatever he says.

Nearby were six stone water jars and each one could hold twenty to thirty gallons of water. These jars were used for people to wash and prepare for the celebration. It was a lot of water. Jesus told the servants to fill the jars. Then he told them to draw some out and take it to the master of ceremonies. They did so and when the master of ceremonies drank it, he was stunned. He didn't know where this had come from, the servants did, but he didn't. He called the groom over and told him, "Most people serve the best wine first and then the cheaper wine when everyone has had too much to drink. You, though, have saved the best wine for now."

Jesus' first miracle was done in relative obscurity. The servants knew what had happened. The disciples knew and put their faith in him. Jesus and his mother knew, but that's about it. Why is that the case? This miracle wasn't done to draw attention to Jesus. It wasn't performed to illustrate his power. It wasn't done to be seen by men. It was done to help some friends get out of a tight spot.

What Does this Mean?

Wouldn't it be wonderful if our lives were perfect? Can you imagine how it would be if we floated through this life without a problem, mistake or fear? I guess that would be great, but I really don't know. I suspect you don't know either. People have problems. Mankind makes mistakes. Marriages are not perfect, and relationships can grow stale. Not every decision that is made is done with the right deliberation and consideration. Angry words get spoken far more often than encouraging ones. Momentary lapses in judgment soil reputations that were years in the making.

What do we do when we find ourselves in the tight spots of life? We're as stuck as the puppy Jazz and as helpless. There is no easy answer, but remember, his grace is greater than the pain of our awkward moments. Jesus cared then and cares now for people who find themselves in the painful predicaments of life. He is concerned about people whose heads are stuck in the bars and wondering how in the world they're ever going to get out. He knows what you're facing. He understands what it is you're up against. He can help you. He can either fix the problem or fix how you look at the problem. His grace is there for you just as it was for an unnamed couple who may have never known the gift he gave them at their wedding.

Maybe you need that today. Maybe you need to be reminded that no situation is too hard for the Lord and that no tight spot is too tough for him to help. As problems present themselves, remember you're surrounded by grace.

Questions
1. What does the fact that Jesus was invited to the wedding tell us about his character?
2. Can you think of any awkward or difficult times in which Jesus was able to help you get through? Describe how that made you feel? What does that say about Jesus' love for you?
3. Do you think most people recognize that Jesus is there for them? Why or why not?
4. How would you describe the connection between love and grace?

Suggested Songs or Hymns
"Amazing Grace" in any of its forms; traditional or any of the contemporary versions
"Mercy Is Falling"
"Grace, Grace, God's Grace"
"Your Grace Is Enough"
"Oh, Glorious Day"

Lesson 2

Grace to Overcome What Was

Lesson Objective: At the end of the lesson each of the participants will understand that Jesus knows about our past mistakes and, if we truly seek him, he can forgive and give us a chance at a new start.

Prayer Focus: Pray that each one in your study group comes to terms with his/her own past and mistakes. May each one allow Jesus to change him/her and may they drink deeply of the living water that he alone offers.

Scripture Reference: John 4:4-26
But he had to go through Samaria. So he came to a Samaritan city called Sychar, near the plot of ground that Jacob had given to his son Joseph. Jacob's well was there, and Jesus, tired out by his journey, was sitting by the well. It was about noon. A Samaritan woman came to draw water, and Jesus said to her, "Give me a drink." (His disciples had gone to the city to buy food.) The Samaritan woman said to him, "How is it that you, a Jew, ask a drink of me, a woman of Samaria?" (Jews do not share things in common with Samaritans.) Jesus answered her, "If you knew the gift of God, and who it is that is saying to you, 'Give me a drink,' you would have asked him, and he would have given you living water." The woman said to him, "Sir, you have no bucket, and the well is deep. Where do you get that living water? Are you greater than our ancestor Jacob, who gave us the well, and with his sons and his flocks drank from it?" Jesus said to her, "Everyone who drinks of this water will be

thirsty again, but those who drink of the water that I will give them will never be thirsty. The water that I will give will become in them a spring of water gushing up to eternal life." The woman said to him, "Sir, give me this water, so that I may never be thirsty or have to keep coming here to draw water." Jesus said to her, "Go, call your husband, and come back." The woman answered him, "I have no husband." Jesus said to her, "You are right in saying, 'I have no husband'; for you have had five husbands, and the one you have now is not your husband. What you have said is true!" The woman said to him, "Sir, I see that you are a prophet. Our ancestors worshiped on this mountain, but you say that the place where people must worship is in Jerusalem." Jesus said to her, "Woman, believe me, the hour is coming when you will worship the Father neither on this mountain nor in Jerusalem. You worship what you do not know; we worship what we know, for salvation is from the Jews. But the hour is coming, and is now here, when the true worshipers will worship the Father in spirit and truth, for the Father seeks such as these to worship him. God is spirit, and those who worship him must worship in spirit and truth." The woman said to him, "I know that Messiah is coming" (who is called Christ). "When he comes, he will proclaim all things to us." Jesus said to her, "I am he, the one who is speaking to you."

The Devil Tries to Use the Past Against You

Comedian Flip Wilson was famous for his saying, "The devil made me do it." It was a catch-phrase that has been used by a lot of people to humorously excuse poor choices or just bad behavior. I suppose that most people that use that line don't exactly mean it in a literal sense. The Bible tells us that the devil can only tempt us. He can't actually *make* someone do something. It seems to me, though, that God does thwart the devil's plans. Consider this godly woman's story:

An elderly lady was well-known for her faith and for her boldness in talking about it. One of the things she was known for was how she would stand on her front porch and shout "Praise the Lord!" Next door to her lived an atheist who would get so angry at her proclamations he would shout, "There ain't no Lord!"

Hard times set in on the elderly lady, and she prayed for God to send her some assistance. She stood on her porch and shouted "Praise the Lord! God, I need groceries and I need them right away! Please. Amen!" Her atheist neighbor heard her prayer.

The next morning the lady went out on her porch and noted a large bag of groceries and shouted, "Praise the Lord!"

The neighbor jumped from behind a bush and said, "Aha! I told you there was no Lord. I bought those groceries, God didn't."

The lady started jumping up and down and clapping her hands and said, "Praise the Lord! He not only sent me groceries, but he made the devil pay for them. Praise the Lord!"

God often takes what the devil intends to use as a weapon or tool against us and makes it into an opportunity to demonstrate his glory. One of the weapons Satan relishes using is a person's past. He likes to remind people of their past, to remind them of how unworthy and sinful they are. A lot of people on this journey through life are accompanied by an uninvited companion; guilt. He shows up at the most inopportune times and brings up difficult and painful issues. Guilt likes to talk about things like…

— the separation and divorce
— the argument with the parent

— the fight with the young-adult child

— the infidelity that happened a decade ago

— the missed opportunities to stand up for what was right

— the bad choices made before your life was different

He wants to instill in you that because of what's happened, you are worthless, hopeless and broken. He and his master hope that you will become shackled by the past so that you are paralyzed in the present and forfeit your future.

In the lesson text for today we meet a woman whose past life was messed up, leaving her without much hope. The tenderness with which Jesus spoke to her and the grace he ministered made a big difference in her life and in her town. It changed things for all of them. It can for you too.

An Old Hatred

Chapter 4 begins with the Pharisees becoming concerned that Jesus' ministry is growing, even larger than John's. Jesus hears of this and decides to travel north to Galilee. Unlike most Jews of his day, though, Jesus decides to go north on the most direct route; through Samaria. Most Jews didn't do that. They made the journey north the long way, going around Samaria. Why? It was simple to them. No self-respecting Jew would have anything to do with Samaritans. The roots of this division were old and deep. The hatred and separation dated all the way back to the days of the patriarchs. Jacob had twelve sons, whose descendants became twelve tribes. Joseph, his favorite, was despised by the other brothers, and they attempted to do away with him. But God intervened and not only preserved Joseph's life, but used him to preserve the lives of the entire family. Before his death, Jacob gave Joseph a blessing in which he called him a "fruitful bough by a well." The blessing was fulfilled, as the territory allotted to the tribes of Joseph's two sons, Ephraim and Manasseh, was the land that eventually became Samaria.

Later, Israel divided into two kingdoms. The northern kingdom, called Israel, established its capital first at Shechem, a revered site in Jewish history, and later at the hilltop city of Samaria. In 722 BC, Assyria conquered Israel and took most of its people into captivity. The Assyrians then brought in Gentile colonists "from Babylon, Cuthah, Ava, Hamath, and from Sepharvaim" to resettle the land. The foreigners brought with them their idols, which the remaining Jews began to worship alongside the God of Israel. They also intermarried.

The southern kingdom of Judah fell to Babylon in 600 BC. Its people, too, were carried off into captivity. But 70 years later, a remnant of 43,000 was permitted to return and rebuild Jerusalem. The people who now inhabited the former northern kingdom, the Samaritans, opposed this and tried to undermine the attempt to reestablish the nation. The full-blooded, monotheistic Jews detested the mixed marriages and worship of their northern cousins. Thus, the walls of bitterness were built on both sides and did nothing but harden for the next 550 years.

Jesus' Divine Appointment

Jesus, though, as we note in verse 4 *had to go* through Samaria. Why? It's possible that he simply had to because of the geographic proximity of Samaria to Galilee, but there's likely more to it. It may well be that a divine appointment had to be kept in the little town of Sychar.

As Jesus entered Sychar with his disciples, he was tired from the journey. He sat down by a well in the middle of town while the disciples went to find food. As he is sitting there, a woman approaches him. It's about the sixth hour of the day, which is an unusual time for a woman to come to the well, but there she was. Maybe she was not welcomed to come at more normal hours. Maybe she wasn't wanted in the crowd of other women. Maybe she just needed the water then. We don't know for sure. However, verse 7 notes for us the incredible and unusual thing that Jesus did. What does it say? "Jesus said to her…" Did you catch that? Jesus spoke to her. We know the rest of the verse indicates that he asked her for a drink, but the very fact that he spoke to her at all was remarkable. Rabbis didn't talk to women as a general rule. No doubt the woman was stunned. She replies to Jesus' request in such a manner. Jesus, however, digs deeper. He tells her that if she knew who was asking for a drink, she would ask him for a drink of living water. Now the woman is really perplexed. Perhaps she looks around, surmising the situation. She notices the obvious. "Sir, you have no bucket, and the well is deep. Where do you get that living water?" Jesus continues this lesson. "Everyone who drinks of this water will be thirsty again, but those who drink of the water that I will give them will never be thirsty. The water that I will give will become in them a spring of water gushing up to eternal life." It's a bold claim and the woman is interested. She wants this living water. She needs it. "Sir, give me this water, so that I may never be thirsty or have to keep coming here to draw water." Jesus, then, gets right to the heart of the matter by getting to the heart of this woman. "Go, call your husband, and come back." We can only imagine the woman's thoughts. There isn't much space in the Bible between verses 16 and 17, but there may have been an awkward silence. She answers his request. "I have no husband." Jesus acknowledges her honesty. "You are right in saying, 'I have no husband'; for you have had five husbands, and the one you have now is not your husband. What you have said is true!" The woman replies to Jesus' declaration in a way that is, perhaps, an understatement. "Sir, I see that you are a prophet."

Compassion Displayed

Let's pause in the story for a moment to consider what's happened. Jesus is in a place where no good Jew would go. He's having a spiritual conversation with a woman. This is a woman who's had a tough life. A woman in that time and culture was expected to marry and have children. Her security and her worth were often dependent on it. Many people, upon reading this text, believe her to be a woman of questionable morals. It's certainly possible. It may be that she is in a sinful relationship. Perhaps her five husbands died, leaving her a widow. Maybe one or more of the marriages ended in divorce. It could be that she's in a sinful sexual relationship with a man that's not her husband or that this last man she's with is one who has simply taken her in because she had no other place to go. Whatever the case may be, it is obvious that this woman's past has been a painful series of events.

Notice what Jesus doesn't do. He doesn't angrily condemn her. He doesn't ignore her as if she is no one. He doesn't do any of the things that religious people would do. While Satan may want to convince this woman she's worthless, Jesus ignores all of that. Her past may well be one sad thing after another, but Jesus refuses to dwell on what was. He reaches out to her in love. He talks of what can be. He shows her compassion, mercy, and grace. Acts of compassion and restoration always move us.

Joseph W. Clifton was thirty-seven when he enlisted as a private in the Union army in August 1861. He was much older than most of the men he fought with, yet like many of his comrades, Clifton probably enlisted out of patriotism, a need for money or merely to escape the doldrums of daily life. At home in the South Jersey town of Burlington, he was the father of five children, and he worked as a stonemason. Serving in the sixth New Jersey Volunteer Infantry, Clifton fought with the Army of the Potomac during the Peninsula Campaign of 1862. As the summer months grew hotter and the combat became more strenuous, Clifton suffered under Virginia's oppressive heat and humidity. Writing from Harrison's Landing, just southeast of Richmond, Clifton described the battles to his brother. But if the fighting was not bad enough, it was horrible to walk through the fields and see only dead soldiers. The experience had a profound impact on the green volunteer. "I never want to see any more fighting for I am sick of it now," he wrote. He wanted to go home to see his family. "I have got another little girl that I never seen yet," he added despondently. Eventually, because of intense pain in his stomach and side, army surgeons sent Clifton to a military hospital in Chester, Pennsylvania. After about four months of recuperation, he decided to take what in Civil War days was called a French leave. On December 5, 1862, Clifton left the hospital without permission. Instead of reporting back to his unit, he went home to Burlington to work and be with his family. Around July 17, 1863, he was arrested and returned to his regiment. Less than a week later he again deserted, this time "while in pursuit of the enemy," as the army was "hourly expecting an engagement." In October he was captured a second time. Two months later, he was court-martialed and found guilty of desertion. He was sentenced to be shot. The commanding general, George Meade, approved the court's decision and set the execution date for January 29, 1864.

Many people intervened and wrote to President Lincoln about Clifton. Lincoln seemed uncertain of what to do. He'd pardoned many, but pardons were bad for morale, especially pardons for desertion. On April 13, 1865, one day before he was shot and killed by John Wilkes Booth, Abraham Lincoln made his decision. A paper was presented in the military court in Clifton's home town. There were no words on the paper other than the signature of A Lincoln, the date and the simple word *Pardoned*. (Jonathan White "The Good and Kind Heart of Lincoln," *The New Jersey Monthly*, February 18, 2014).

It's an incredible act of compassion on the part of a president. It's an act that cries out no matter what happened yesterday, I believe in you today and have hope for tomorrow. For Joseph Clifton, it meant a new life.

A New Life

Jesus continues talking to her, explaining the nature of true worship. She understands what he means as he says, "a time is coming" and states plainly, "I know that Messiah is coming." Jesus tells her directly in verse 26, "I am he." As he says this, the disciples return, and they are shocked to see this conversation taking place. Jesus, though, is at the crucial part of the discussion. The woman makes a decision to accept Jesus for who he is. She has found one man in whom she can trust. She's found a man who knows her bitter story, but talks of hope and life. She leaves her water jar and runs to tell everyone who'll listen about the man who told her everything she'd ever done. The Messiah has come to Sychar!

This woman got a chance at new life. Her past would no longer rob her of a future. The town got a revival. Samaritans encountered the Messiah, the one for whom their fathers looked and longed. The disciples got a lesson in racial sensitivity and Jesus, well, I don't know if he ever got a drink, but he certainly gained followers.

When we're reminded about our past and how it is not all that it should be, remember a woman of Samaria. Remember a thirsty Jesus who came to her for a drink and gave her life and a future. He'll come to you, too. Grace to overcome what was. Is there any of us who doesn't need it? Is there any of us who doesn't want it?

Questions

1. Why do you think Jesus "had to" go through Samaria?

2. What do you think the woman thought as Jesus spoke to her? What does this tell us about Jesus?

3. Jesus knew about this woman's past and her present situation. Do you think he knows what is going on in your life? Does he know the details of where you've been and what you've done?

4. This woman seemed to be ready for "living water." She went and told everyone she could find about Jesus. Do you think there is an excitement when people first encounter Jesus? Where does it go?

Suggested Songs or Hymns

"Jesus Paid It All"
"Not Guilty"
"Mighty To Save"
"Blessed Redeemer"
"You Alone Can Rescue"
"You Are My King"

Grace for the Times When Life's Too Hard

Lesson Objective: At the end of this lesson, each of the participants will be able to identify the presence of Jesus when life's demands are overwhelming and allow him to bring comfort against a backdrop of frustration and calm in the middle of chaos.

Prayer Focus: Pray that each of the participants in the group will be able to set aside the frantic pace of this life and the heavy burdens that they may be carrying and sit in the presence of the one who calms the storms. Pray for peace for all who gather in this study.

Scripture Reference: John 6:1-24
After this Jesus went to the other side of the Sea of Galilee, also called the Sea of Tiberias. A large crowd kept following him, because they saw the signs that he was doing for the sick. Jesus went up the mountain and sat down there with his disciples. Now the Passover, the festival of the Jews, was near. When he looked up and saw a large crowd coming toward him, Jesus said to Philip, "Where are we to buy bread for these people to eat?" He said this to test him, for he himself knew what he was going to do. Philip answered him, "Six months' wages would not buy enough bread for each of them to get a little." One of his disciples, Andrew, Simon Peter's brother, said to him, "There is a boy here who has five barley loaves and two fish. But what are they among

so many people?" Jesus said, "Make the people sit down." Now there was a great deal of grass in the place; so they sat down, about five thousand in all. Then Jesus took the loaves, and when he had given thanks, he distributed them to those who were seated; so also the fish, as much as they wanted. When they were satisfied, he told his disciples, "Gather up the fragments left over, so that nothing may be lost." So they gathered them up, and from the fragments of the five barley loaves, left by those who had eaten, they filled twelve baskets. When the people saw the sign that he had done, they began to say, "This is indeed the prophet who is to come into the world." When Jesus realized that they were about to come and take him by force to make him king, he withdrew again to the mountain by himself.

When evening came, his disciples went down to the sea, got into a boat, and started across the sea to Capernaum. It was now dark, and Jesus had not yet come to them. The sea became rough because a strong wind was blowing. When they had rowed about three or four miles, they saw Jesus walking on the sea and coming near the boat, and they were terrified. But he said to them, "It is I; do not be afraid." Then they wanted to take him into the boat, and immediately the boat reached the land toward which they were going.

The next day the crowd that had stayed on the other side of the sea saw that there had been only one boat there. They also saw that Jesus had not got into the boat with his disciples, but that his disciples had gone away alone. Then some boats from Tiberias came near the place where they had eaten the bread after the Lord had given thanks. So when the crowd saw that neither Jesus nor his disciples were there, they themselves got into the boats and went to Capernaum looking for Jesus.

Things Are Not Always as They Seem

Sometimes things aren't what they appear to be. The little girl was eight years old when her family moved to a new house and she finally got her own bedroom. She wouldn't have to share a bedroom with her older sister and she was excited, though her older sister might have been a bit more excited than she was. She couldn't have been more enthusiastic as she helped her mom decorate the room, choose the wallpaper, bedspread and curtains. At last the room was ready. It was a beautiful room and a tribute to the wonderful world of princesses. The night finally came; her first night in her own room. She was so looking forward to it. She even took her bath early to get to be in *her* room. Her mom and dad both tucked her in. They prayed with her and kissed her goodnight. They left her room, turned off the light and closed the door. The nightlight gave a tiny glow to the dark room. She lay in her bed quietly. That's when it happened. She heard a noise. Then she heard another one. *What was that! It's getting closer. It sounds like it's in the closet.* She sat up and looked around her room. What was once a warm princess party was now dark and scary. Then she saw it. It was in the corner. It was casting a big shadow that seemed to be getting bigger by the second. With the growing shadow and the noise, she couldn't take it anymore. She cried out to her mom and dad. They came rushing in.

Most parents have experienced this story or a version of it. The noise that seems so menacing is nothing more than the clock on the wall. The growing shadow is just that of a giant stuffed bear. In the light, it seems so harmless. In the dark, though, things can sure look different.

We can't always go by how something looks. There are some days when things are going well. However, there are times when we are drowning in the churning waters of work, chores, responsibilities and just the tiresome garbage that everyday life throws at us. It's during those times that we feel as if we can't go on. *I've had it! I'm done* becomes our two-pronged mantra. What do we do when we're going under for the final time? Is there any hope? Life's problems can sometimes look too difficult to solve and too menacing to handle. Jesus knew what it was like to be overwrought with the stuff of life. On a hectic, frantic day we see him show grace to a hungry, insistent crowd and frightened disciples. Let's take a look at the sixth chapter of John.

An Impossible Situation

The sixth chapter begins with Jesus, after telling the crowds that he was the "bread of life," crossing the Sea of Galilee with his disciples. A huge crowd of people have followed him. Word is spreading about the miracles he's doing. That leads to the first stressful situation that Jesus encountered on this day.

After teaching and preaching, Jesus looks out at the mass of humanity before him and asks Philip, "Where do we buy bread for these people to eat?" He knew what he was going to do, but he wanted to see what Philip would say. Can you imagine what Philip may have thought? Perhaps he gulped, looked around and finally blurted out, "Eight months wages wouldn't buy enough bread for each one to have a bite!" Andrew, another of Jesus' disciples, has been listening and watching. He's got a different answer. "Here's a boy with five small barely loaves and two fish, but what's that among so many?" The disciples have no good answer for the food problem.

Jesus, though, has an answer. He tells them to make the people sit. He prays and he begins to hand out food from this small lunch. You know the story. Five thousand men, plus women and children, ate as much as they wanted with twelve baskets of leftovers. That's the part we know pretty well. What comes next sometimes gets overlooked.

Not the Right Time

Jesus' second stressful situation comes from an impatient crowd. The people are impressed with this miracle. They begin talking among themselves about who this Jesus really is. Jesus picks up on what's going on and understands that they want to force him to be king. This isn't the right time, and this isn't the right way. Jesus withdraws from the crowd that clamors for him and chants his name. He goes away by himself among the rocks of the mountain. He defies the logic of every public relations expert and avoids the masses that cheer him.

The day is drawing to a close. Jesus is up on the mountain, alone. The disciples, after the busy afternoon of serving lunch, get into a boat and head out across the lake. They are headed for Capernaum. It's dark now and Jesus isn't with them. A strong wind begins blowing; the sea is rolling and just trying to row the boat becomes an impossible task. They've rowed three or three and a half miles out into the lake and it's now late. The wind is really blowing and the opposite shore seems far away.

Problem on the Lake

Jesus' disciples are in trouble and Jesus faces a third stressful moment. We get the sense that he's aware of what's going on with his disciples. He comes to them, walking on the water. Naturally, they are surprised at this and think he's a ghost. In the face of hard, opposing winds, darkness and physical exhaustion, Jesus tells them, "It is I; do not be afraid." The disciples take him into the boat and immediately the boat reaches the shore where they were headed. The next day, the crowd back on the other shore realized that Jesus was gone, but only one boat had left and Jesus wasn't in it. Others come from Tiberias to the place where they'd eaten, but Jesus and the disciples are not there. The crowds then go to Capernaum in search of Jesus.

Responses to Stress
Before we leave this story, let's look back at the three stressful events in this one day of Jesus' life and notice what he did and what he offered.

Trust
Upon first glance, it seemed Jesus had the problem of inadequate resources. There wasn't enough food for the people to eat. There are times when we feel like we have the problem of inadequate resources, too. We find ourselves saying things like, *"Lord, there isn't enough money for..."* or *"I don't have enough time, patience, ability..."* Thinking we don't have what we need to do what needs to be done is scary.

What did Jesus do about the apparent lack of resources? Let's note, right away, that what looked like a problem really wasn't. There is no such thing as "not enough" when it concerns Jesus.

Faith the size of a mustard seed can move a mountain.

One exclamation from an outcast leper brought healing.

Last words from a dying thief brought the promise of paradise.

One lunch fed a multitude.

Jesus prayed and began dividing the food. When what we've got doesn't seem to match what we need, turn to Jesus. Pray. Trust him. The power, the goodness, the grace of Jesus that has so often taken so little and made so much can help you too.

When Hudson Taylor went to China, he made the voyage on a sailing vessel. As it neared the channel between the southern Malay Peninsula and the island of Sumatra, the missionary heard an urgent knock on his stateroom door. He opened it, and there stood the captain of the ship.

"Mr. Taylor," he said, "we have no wind. We are drifting toward an island where the people are heathen, and I fear they are cannibals."

"What can I do?" asked Taylor.

"I understand that you believe in God. I want you to pray for wind."

"All right, Captain, I will, but you must set the sail."

"Why that's ridiculous! There's not even the slightest breeze. Besides, the sailors will think I'm crazy."

But finally, because of Taylor's insistence, he agreed. Three quarters of an hour later he returned and found the missionary still on his knees.

"You can stop praying now," said the captain. "We've got more wind than we know what to do with!"

God provided more than enough wind for Hudson Taylor and his fellow shipmates. God provided more than enough food for a hungry multitude. God will provide what you need when you need it. Trust him. Trust his goodness. Look for his grace.

Time Alone with God

Jesus also faced the stress of dealing with people who had unreal or unfounded expectations. He had a crowd that wanted him to be king. They were planning to force the issue. What did he do? He withdrew from them. He got away and prayed. There's a lesson there for us, too. When the demands of the people around us are so insistent and intense, we need time away from them and time alone with the Lord.

William Wilberforce, Christian statesman of Great Britain in the late eighteenth and early nineteenth centuries, once said, "I must secure more time for private devotions. I have been living far too public for me. The shortening of private devotions starves the soul. It grows lean and faint."

Don't Be Afraid

Jesus' disciples were in a precarious situation. They were on the lake and the storm was fierce. They were having a hard time getting across. Jesus was aware of their plight. We get that, too, don't we? We know what it's like to have a friend or a loved one hurting and struggling. How many parents have lost sleep worked up over the plight of their child? How many husbands or wives have agonized as their spouse has suffered? We know what it's like when we're in that crucible moment. When those times come, and they do, see what Jesus did. He came to his disciples in their distress and told them "It is I. Do not be afraid." He came to them. Note that. Those were comforting words through the uncertain winds and strain. Those words can comfort today.

When the medical report is not good, hear the words, "It is I. Do not be afraid."

When your heart is broken and it seems like the sun won't ever shine again, hear the calm voice, "It is I. Do not be afraid."

When help seems far away and you're all alone, hear the quiet voice from the shadows; "It is I. Do not be afraid."

When the stack of bills is higher than the stack of money and fear, like a vise, grips your heart, listen as he says, "It is I. Do not be afraid."

Stressful situations did not faze Jesus on this tough day. They don't have to cause us anguish, either. Looking to Jesus' example can be an encouragement. We can know that no matter how tough the situation might be, Jesus will not leave us to deal with it alone. We can have peace in predicament. We are offered hope when hassled. We are given confidence despite conflict. No matter how grim things may look, grace reminds us that he is there.

Questions

1. What things cause stress in our lives? Why does this happen?

2. With regard to stressful situations, why is it hard to trust that God/Jesus can make a difference? What do we tend to look at rather than at him?

3. Is it hard for you to find time alone with God? Why prevents that from happening? How might you be able to better do it?

4. People sometimes have so many issues and struggles that fear seems to be the natural outcome of it. How can we not be afraid? What helps drive out fear?

Suggested Songs or Hymns

"You Are Good"
"Trust And Obey"
"O, No, You Never Let Go"
"I Lift Up My Hands"
"I Surrender All"

Lesson 4

Grace for the Broken Heart

Lesson Objective: At the end of the lesson, each of the participants will know and understand that Jesus Christ cares for him/her, especially when things are tough.

Prayer Focus: Pray that each one in the group might find God's grace expressed in Jesus Christ to be a healing and restorative force.

Scripture Reference: John 11:17-44

When Jesus arrived, he found that Lazarus had already been in the tomb four days. Now Bethany was near Jerusalem, some two miles away, and many of the Jews had come to Martha and Mary to console them about their brother. When Martha heard that Jesus was coming, she went and met him, while Mary stayed at home. Martha said to Jesus, "Lord, if you had been here, my brother would not have died. But even now I know that God will give you whatever you ask of him." Jesus said to her, "Your brother will rise again." Martha said to him, "I know that he will rise again in the resurrection on the last day." Jesus said to her, "I am the resurrection and the life. Those who believe in me, even though they die, will live, and everyone who lives and believes in me will never die. Do you believe this?" She said to him, "Yes, Lord, I believe that you are the Messiah, the Son of God, the one coming into the world."

When she had said this, she went back and called her sister Mary, and told her privately, "The Teacher is here and is calling for you." And when she heard it, she got up quickly and went to him. Now Jesus had not yet come to the village, but was still at the place where Martha had met him. The Jews who were with her in the house, consoling her, saw Mary get up quickly and go out. They followed her because they thought that she was going to the tomb to weep there. When Mary came where Jesus was and saw him, she knelt at his feet and said to him, "Lord, if you had been here, my brother would not have died." When Jesus saw her weeping, and the Jews who came with her also weeping, he was greatly disturbed in spirit and deeply moved. He said, "Where have you laid him?" They said to him, "Lord, come and see." Jesus began to weep. So the Jews said, "See how he loved him!" But some of them said, "Could not he who opened the eyes of the blind man have kept this man from dying?"

Then Jesus, again greatly disturbed, came to the tomb. It was a cave, and a stone was lying against it. Jesus said, "Take away the stone." Martha, the sister of the dead man, said to him, "Lord, already there is a stench because he has been dead four days." Jesus said to her, "Did I not tell you that if you believed, you would see the glory of God?" So they took away the stone. And Jesus looked upward and said, "Father, I thank you for having heard me. I knew that you always hear me, but I have said this for the sake of the crowd standing here, so that they may believe that you sent me." 4 When he had said this, he cried with a loud voice, "Lazarus, come out!" The dead man came out, his hands and feet bound with strips of cloth, and his face wrapped in a cloth. Jesus said to them, "Unbind him, and let him go."

An Uncomfortable Feeling

The summer after my senior year of high school I had the opportunity to work for one of our local funeral homes. I know that sounds unusual for a summer job just out of high school, but it was pretty good money and a great learning experience. While there I saw nearly fifty funerals and how people interacted and dealt with grief and loss. I also washed and waxed a lot of cars and cut grass!

There was one part of the job that I especially remember. Every now and then I would be asked to go the hospital to pick up a body. I didn't do it often, usually the morticians themselves did that, but when they were busy or weren't around, they'd ask me. I remember one time specifically. I drove to one of our city's hospitals in the company station wagon and parked in the back, near the door closest to the morgue. The hospital was doing some renovations at the time, so there were several members of a construction crew working at that part of the building. Let me paint this picture for you. I was an eighteen-year-old just out of high school and not too tough looking. These construction workers were, well, construction workers. On a normal day these guys wouldn't have noticed a guy like me in the slightest. On this day, though, it was incredibly different. On my way in and especially on my way out these tough, hardened guys looked away, almost in fear. I'm sure it was an uncomfortable feeling for them and one they were not expecting to see in their work day.

I suppose, though, death is like that. We know it's out there, but we aren't really comfortable with it and we certainly resent it intruding upon our regular day. We often struggle with the word itself. The word death isn't one that we use a lot. We have a tendency to soften our language when someone has died. We say things like "they've passed on," "they passed away," or "they went to be with the Lord." The words "death" and "died" are scary. They are so permanent; so final. If ever there was a place for grace, it has to be at the hospital bed of one taking his/her final breaths. If grace is real, it has to be real in the cemetery. If grace is going to be sufficient, then it needs to be strong enough to hold up the broken heart.

It Wasn't Supposed to Be Like This

Mary and Martha were in need of grace. They stood at the intersection of disappointment and despair. Four days earlier they sent a message to Jesus. His friend, their brother, Lazarus, was sick and dying. They pleaded with Jesus to come. They expected him to come. When he heard of Lazarus' illness and the sisters' desire that he come, inexplicably, he waited two days before leaving. Then, when he announced his intention to go because Lazarus had fallen asleep, the disciples told him that he shouldn't. If Lazarus was sleeping, he'd get better and, besides, the Jews there had tried to stone him. But while Jesus and the disciples waited, discussed and finally came, the unthinkable happened. Lazarus died. He'd been in the grave four days when Martha meets Jesus on the road. It's hard when things don't go as we hope they will.

A close friend has an aunt who, after months of proving a worthy adversary, appears to be succumbing to an increasingly debilitating bout with cancer. Unfortunately, many of the familiar signs are there — the inhumanity of late night emergency room visits... extended periods without the consumption of food... blurred lines of reality... and occasional exclamations of 'being so tired'. And for loved ones, the overwhelming feelings of helplessness, frustration, sorrow, anger and fear continue to grow. Teary eyes bore witness to a grueling, yet unsatisfied search for answers.

I think Mary and Martha knew what this friend was experiencing. It's a strenuous search for answers trying to understand why those we love hurt, suffer and die. A broken heart can hurt all over.

Jesus Understands

Jesus understands the pain of a broken heart, but just as the pain is real, so is grace. In Jesus' reactions to Mary and Martha there are some important lessons.

Certainty of the Resurrection

First, notice in this text that Jesus spoke words of absolute certainty. He told Martha just after hearing from her, "Lord, if had you been here my brother would not have died," these words of assurance. "Your brother will rise again." There was no hesitation or stammering. It was a simple declaration of truth. Martha recognized it as truth and told Jesus that she believed he would rise again, too, at the resurrection. Martha was well-versed in what the Pharisees taught about the resurrection being a reality, but Jesus wanted her to move from believing a teaching, to trusting a person. He told her, "I am the resurrection and the life. Those who believe in me, even though they die, will live, and everyone who lives and believes in me will never die." He then makes it a direct challenge; "Do you believe this?" That's the crux of the matter, isn't it? *Do you believe this?*

That's the whole point of grace, Lent and Easter. The historical evidence is there. The Bible lays out in detail the events of Jesus' life. The critical question is one of belief. It's an individual choice that must be made. Martha had to make it. Mary did, too. And so do you.

The message of the empty tomb is foreshadowed in this account. The grave is not the final destination and for those who know and love Jesus Christ, death need not be feared.

Know that He Cares

Second, Jesus demonstrates love, compassion and caring. In a verse that children throughout church history have memorized as one of the shortest in the English New Testament comes a compelling and striking story. "Jesus began to weep." These are simple words that speak of a wonderful spiritual truth.

Why did Jesus weep? He didn't weep because Lazarus was dead and gone. He knew what he was about to do. I don't think he wept because of the grip that death has on his people. He's about to demonstrate how fragile that hold really is. I think his weeping has a lot to do with the fact that Jesus knows, understands and cares about the pain that his friends feel and are going through. What hurts them hurts him. I think he's also weeping because the stench of Satan's work soils the lives of those he loves. He is about to reverse this death, but even for a moment, seeing the fingerprints of Satan on the lives of those he loves breaks his heart and drives him to weep. Things were not supposed to be like this and that brings tears to his eyes. I think he weeps because people matter to him and when they're sad, it touches him. The simple truth that Jesus wept brings comfort, encouragement and hope. When we weep, we do not weep alone. Jesus is there and because he is, there is purpose to our struggle.

A man visited an orange grove where an irrigation pump had broken down. The season was unusually dry and some of the trees were beginning to die for lack of water. The man giving the tour then took the fellow to his own orchard where irrigation was used sparingly. "These trees could go without rain for another two weeks," he said. "You see, when they were young, I frequently kept water from them. This hardship caused them to send their roots deeper into the soil in search of moisture. Now mine are the deepest-rooted trees in the area. While others are being scorched by the sun, these are finding moisture at a greater depth."

Times of sadness and brokenness allows us to "send our roots deeper" into Jesus Christ. There we find the comfort of his grace.

Jesus Has Power

A final statement of Jesus bears looking at in this passage. He has been brought to the tomb of Lazarus. Everyone is there; Martha, Mary, the Jews from around that region. Sadness is everywhere. Satan's finest work is on display. A loved-one is dead and buried behind a stone. Hope is gone. Bitterness, sorrow and frustration rule the day. Into that dreary scene Jesus boldly marches. He tells them to move the stone. It's a strange request. Martha, ever practical, speaks up. "Lord, already there is a stench because he has been dead four days." Unpleasant, unseemly and unusual; but Jesus is firm in his demand. "Did I not tell you that if you believed, you would see the glory of God?" The stone is removed. We can imagine the wide eyes peering into the darkness of the death cave. We can see the mouths and noses covered with cloth, anticipating the stench. Jesus, though, looks up to heaven and prays. He knows what he and his father are about to do. He acknowledges that he is praying for the benefit of those around him. Then, in words, the echo throughout history, he cries, "Lazarus, come out!" Can you imagine the shudder that went through the crowd? They've seen miracles before, perhaps, but this, well, this is incredible. Necks may have been straining to catch a glimpse of what was going on in the darkness of the tomb. *Was that a noise? Did someone see a shadow? Here he comes! He's alive!*

Lazarus, still wrapped in grave clothes, stepped forth from the darkness of death. Jesus gave the order, "Unbind him and let him go." Death is swallowed up in victory!

This story is one that resounds with grace. There is a certainty about what Jesus has promised. Trusting him will lead to life. There is an empathy that bathes all that Jesus does. He does understand and he does care. There is power in what Jesus can do. He is greater than that which seeks to bring us down.

Understand this Important Truth

This comes, however, with a caution. Lazarus rose from the dead, but he did die again later. Jesus can and sometimes does the miraculous. The sick are healed, and the broken are completely restored. Sometimes, though, the grace he provides is the strength to get through the dark times to a better time. Sometimes the grace is there, not to bring wholeness in this life, but to carry one on to the next one, the real one. Grace is not an insurance policy that nothing bad will ever happen to us in this world. Grace is the promise that whatever happens, we won't be alone. Grace gives us the confidence that nothing this world throws at us will ever really have any lasting effect because our hope is in the Lord. Grace is the reminder that Jesus is stronger than any boogeyman. Sink your roots deeply into his wonderful grace.

Questions
1. What is it about death that makes people uncomfortable?
2. What does it tell us about Mary and Martha that they called for Jesus when Lazarus was sick? What does it say about them when they both acknowledged that had Jesus been there, their brother would not have died?
3. What does it tell us about Jesus that he wept? Why did he weep?
4. Do you think Christians are afraid of death? If so, why? Should they be? Why?

Suggested Songs or Hymns
"I Will Rise"
"There's Power In The Blood"
"In Christ Alone"
"Glorious Day"

Lesson 5

Grace When Things Are Chaotic

Lesson Objective: At the end of the lesson, the participants will understand that God's peace is promised to those who follow Jesus and is available, especially in hard or challenging times.

Prayer Focus: Pray for each of the people in the group that s/he might know the "peace of God which transcends all understanding." Pray that when the chaotic times come, they will find that island of calm in the storm.

Scripture Reference: John 16:17-33

Then some of his disciples said to one another, "What does he mean by saying to us, 'A little while, and you will no longer see me, and again a little while, and you will see me'; and 'Because I am going to the Father'?" They said, "What does he mean by this 'a little while'? We do not know what he is talking about." Jesus knew that they wanted to ask him, so he said to them, "Are you discussing among yourselves what I meant when I said, 'A little while, and you will no longer see me, and again a little while, and you will see me'? Very truly, I tell you, you will weep and mourn, but the world will rejoice; you will have pain, but your pain will turn into joy. When a woman is in labor, she has pain, because her hour has come. But when her child is born, she no longer remembers the anguish because of the joy of having brought a human being into the world. So you have pain now; but I will see you again, and your hearts will rejoice, and no one will take your joy from you. On that day you will ask nothing of me. Very truly, I tell you, if you ask anything of the Father in my name, he will give it to you. Until now you have not asked for anything in my name. Ask and you will receive, so that your joy may be complete.

"I have said these things to you in figures of speech. The hour is coming when I will no longer speak to you in figures, but will tell you plainly of the Father. On that day you will ask in my name. I do not say to you that I will ask the Father on your behalf; for the Father himself loves you, because you have loved me and have believed that I came from God. I came from the Father and have come into the world; again, I am leaving the world and am going to the Father." His disciples said, "Yes, now you are speaking plainly, not in any figure of speech! Now we know that you know all things, and do not need to have anyone question you; by this we believe that you came from God." Jesus answered them, "Do you now believe? The hour is coming, indeed it has come, when you will be scattered, each one to his home, and you will leave me alone. Yet I am not alone because the Father is with me. I have said this to you, so that in me you may have peace. In the world you face persecution. But take courage; I have conquered the world!"

Storms Come

When life is going well and we are facing few problems, it's easy to trust. When God's grace provides us smooth sailing, it's simple to sing "It is well with my soul." What about the times, though, when the sailing is not so smooth? Is grace still there on the choppy seas of life? Searching for peace in life's storms can be a challenge. Maria Snyder wrote in her book *Fire Study*, "There's always another storm. It's the way the world works. Snowstorms, rainstorms, windstorms, sandstorms, and firestorms. Some are fierce, and others are small. You have to deal with each one separately, but you need to keep an eye on what's brewing for tomorrow."

This statement seems about right for life as we experience it, doesn't it? There are times it seems like we just get through one crisis only to find that another part of our lives is in turmoil. Chaos is unsettling and unnerving. We long for peace. We reach out toward an oasis of calm in the desert of confusion and uncertainty. Is there any way that we can have peace in this difficult and frustrating world?

Jesus' disciples were aware of uncertainty and chaos. As Jesus is in the garden, only hours away from his death, he talks to them of what's going to happen next; what he's going to do; what he's leaving them. The words he speaks, *I am leaving; you will see me no more; scattered; alone; trouble;* all of these leave the disciples with an uneasy, uncertain feeling. What will happen to them now? What will it mean for Jesus to go away? What's going to happen to his mission? Unanswered questions allow fear, doubt and nervous feelings to thrive and grow. We understand that we shouldn't worry, shouldn't borrow trouble, but it is so hard in the storms of life to find peace.

What Does Peace Look Like?

An artist was commissioned by a wealthy man to paint something that would depict peace. After a great deal of thought, the artist painted a beautiful country scene. There were green fields with cows standing in them, birds were flying in the blue sky and a lovely little village lay in a distant valley. The artist gave the picture to the man, but there was a look of disappointment on his face. The man said to the artist, "This isn't a picture of true peace. It isn't right. Go back and try again."

The artist went back to his studio, thought for several hours about peace, then went to his canvas and began to paint. When he was finished, there on the canvas was a beautiful picture of a mother, holding a sleeping baby in her arms, smiling lovingly at the child. He thought *surely, this is true peace,* and hurried to give the picture to the wealthy man. But again, the wealthy man refused the painting and asked the painter to try again.

The artist returned again to his studio. He was discouraged, he was tired, and he was disappointed. Anger swelled inside him. He felt the rejection of this wealthy man. Again, he thought, he even prayed for inspiration to paint a picture of true peace. Then an idea came to him. He rushed to the canvas and began to paint as he had never painted before. When he finished, he hurried to the wealthy man.

He gave the painting to the man. He studied it carefully for several minutes. The artist held his breath. Then the wealthy man said, "Now this is a picture of true peace." He accepted the painting, paid the artist and everyone was happy.

And what was this picture of true peace? The picture showed a stormy sea pounding against a cliff. The artist had captured the fury of the wind as it whipped black rain clouds which were laced with streaks of lightening. The sea was roaring in turmoil, waves churning, the dark sky filled with the power of the furious thunderstorm.

And in the middle of the picture, under a cliff, the artist had painted a small bird, safe and dry in her nest snuggled safely in the rocks. The bird was at peace, in the midst of the storm that raged about her. That was true peace.

Peace in the middle of the storm. That's really what having peace is all about, isn't it? That's the message that Jesus is trying to convey to his disciples in his garden prayer and that's what his grace provides. If grace can only get us through the smooth times, it isn't worth much. Jesus shows his disciples how they can have peace when all is chaotic. Let's take a look.

A Hard Teaching

After discussing "A little while, and you will no longer see me, and again a little while, and you will see me" with them and giving them insight into what it means, Jesus lets them know that they will weep and mourn while the world rejoices. He promises, though, that their grief would turn to joy. In this difficult text Jesus is telling the disciples that in a short time he will leave them. He'll be arrested and crucified. They will mourn. The kingdom is not yet established. They will be frightened, and all will seem lost. The world will rejoice that Jesus is no longer around, but his disciples will mourn. However, he also makes it clear that "in a little while" they will see him again. He will rise from the dead. Their grief will turn to joy. It will be an incredible turn.

A Comeback Story

We all like a good comeback story. Sports fans might recall this one. It was the 2004 American League Championship Series. Boston and New York went at it for the right to go to the World Series. The Red Sox looked on course to be humiliated by their greatest rivals as they lost the first three games of the best-of seven series, and trailing by a run in the ninth inning of game four, it looked like it was all over for another year. But an amazing stolen base by Dave Roberts — one of the most famous in baseball history — helped him score a tying run. David Ortiz then smashed a home run for the Red Sox in extra innings to win the game, and the Boston side won the next three games in a row (thanks to another Ortiz home-run in extra innings) to make it to the World Series, where they went on to beat the St Louis Cardinals in four straight games. No one who watched the series could believe how the Sox could come back, or the Yankees choked if you're a New Yorker.

That feeling, in a very small way, is what Jesus is alluding to in this passage. He wants the disciples to know that grief, confusion and chaos may have their day, but it won't last. At the resurrection, the disciples wouldn't have to wonder or ask each other about who Jesus was or what he meant.

God Loves You

Jesus then reminds them of the Father's love for them. He tells them, "The Father himself loves you, because you have loved me and have believed that I came from God." Jesus goes on to tell them that he is going back to the Father. They understand what he's saying and tell him, "Yes, now you are speaking plainly, not in any figure of speech!" They get that he is going back to the Father. They also get that they are loved by the Father and can ask of the Father because of Jesus. That's a significant point. They know that they are loved and can go to God. There is something about being loved that matters.

A young man wrote this to his girlfriend. "Sweetheart, if this world was as hot as the Sahara Desert, I would crawl on my knees through the burning sand to come to you. If the world would be like the Atlantic Ocean, I would swim through shark infested waters to come to you. I would fight the fiercest dragon to be by your side. I will see you on Thursday if it doesn't rain."

Well, he didn't quite get it, but I hope you do. When confusion, uncertainty and doubt are having their way, remember God's love. He loves you. It doesn't, by itself, make these things vanish, but it changes how we look at things. God loves you. It's a cry of hope. It's the harbinger of grace.

Disciples Will Run

Jesus acknowledges the disciples' belief. However, he notes that there will come a time when all of them fall away. Things will get so tough that they will all run, leaving Jesus by himself. We don't know what their response was to this dire prophecy. The Bible doesn't tell us. We are left to speculate. Did they stare at one another in disbelief? Did they try to envision a scenario in which they abandon Jesus or did they just look at each other wondering how it was the guy next to them could do such an awful thing? We just don't know. What we do know, though, is what Jesus said next. Look at verse 33. "I have said this to you, so that in me you may have peace. In the world you face persecution. But take courage; I have conquered the world!" Did you catch what Jesus said in this powerful verse?

Three Lessons

Three things leap from the page. First, he said he was telling them these things that they might have peace. He wanted them to have that calm assurance that no matter how rough the storm raged, they would be able to get through it.

He also told them that in this world, they would have trouble or be persecuted. He made it clear that the world was a turbulent, difficult place. They should expect it to be hard. They should look for it to get rough. They shouldn't be surprised when chaos and confusion made an appearance.

The third thing to notice about this verse is what comes next. Did you catch the exclamation? *But take courage; I have conquered the world!* There is good news. "But" is a conjunction that implies a contrast. There will be trouble in this world, but. That's a good place for that conjunction. Take heart. Be of good cheer. Be of good courage. Why? Jesus tells them. *I have conquered the world.* He is the victor! He is the champion. Nothing the world throws at him will have any "sticking power." Because Jesus has overcome the world, the disciples could also overcome. They need not drown in the waves of doubt, fear and uncertainty. They overcome because Jesus overcame. So can you. God's grace is as present in difficult times as it is when times are good.

Sometimes things look rather bleak. Sometimes the outcome is in doubt. Sometimes you're uncertain and life is chaotic. We feel like we're behind and we're never going to catch up.

A man approached a little league baseball game one afternoon. He asked a boy in the dugout what the score was. The boy responded, "Eighteen to nothing — we're behind." "Boy," said the spectator, "I'll bet you're discouraged." "Why should I be discouraged?" replied the little boy. "We haven't even gotten up to bat yet!"

As long as Jesus is still coming up to bat, the game isn't over. Don't forget that.

Questions
1. Why do the storms of life tend to rob us of our peace? Do you ever wonder why they have to happen? Why do people question God on these things?
2. How would you describe peace? What does it mean to have "God's peace?"
3. The lesson speaks of a Comeback Story. Have you ever experienced a comeback story? What happened? What did it tell you about faith, grace and Jesus?
4. What does it mean to you that Jesus has "conquered the world?" Do you think most Christians live in that victory? Why or why not?

Suggested Songs or Hymns
"It Is Well With My Soul"
"What A Friend We Have In Jesus"
"Perfect Peace"
"Peace Like A River"
"Peace In The Valley"

Lesson 6

Grace on Display

Lesson Objective: At the end of the lesson, each participant will be able to identify and explain the significance of Jesus' death on the cross and connect it to God's plan of grace.

Prayer Focus: Pray that each one in your group understands that Jesus' death on the cross was for him/her personally. May they receive the grace that is freely offered to them.

Scripture Reference: John 19:16-37
Then he handed him over to them to be crucified.
So they took Jesus; and carrying the cross by himself, he went out to what is called The Place of the Skull, which in Hebrew is called Golgotha. There they crucified him, and with him two others, one on either side, with Jesus between them. Pilate also had an inscription written and put on the cross. It read, "Jesus of Nazareth, the King of the Jews." Many of the Jews read this inscription, because the place where Jesus was crucified was near the city; and it was written in Hebrew, in Latin, and in Greek. Then the chief priests of the Jews said to Pilate, "Do not write, 'The King of the Jews,' but, 'This man said, I am King of the Jews.'" Pilate answered, "What I have written I have written." When the soldiers had crucified Jesus, they took his clothes and divided them into four parts, one for each soldier. They also took his tunic; now the tunic was seamless, woven in one piece from the top. So they said to one another, "Let us not tear it, but

cast lots for it to see who will get it." This was to fulfill what the scripture says, "They divided my clothes among themselves, and for my clothing they cast lots." And that is what the soldiers did. Meanwhile, standing near the cross of Jesus were his mother, and his mother's sister, Mary the wife of Clopas, and Mary Magdalene. When Jesus saw his mother and the disciple whom he loved standing beside her, he said to his mother, "Woman, here is your son." Then he said to the disciple, "Here is your mother." And from that hour the disciple took her into his own home. After this, when Jesus knew that all was now finished, he said (in order to fulfill the scripture), "I am thirsty." A jar full of sour wine was standing there. So they put a sponge full of the wine on a branch of hyssop and held it to his mouth. When Jesus had received the wine, he said, "It is finished." Then he bowed his head and gave up his spirit.

Since it was the day of Preparation, the Jews did not want the bodies left on the cross during the Sabbath, especially because that Sabbath was a day of great solemnity. So they asked Pilate to have the legs of the crucified men broken and the bodies removed. Then the soldiers came and broke the legs of the first and of the other who had been crucified with him. But when they came to Jesus and saw that he was already dead, they did not break his legs. Instead, one of the soldiers pierced his side with a spear, and at once blood and water came out. (He who saw this has testified so that you also may believe. His testimony is true, and he knows that he tells the truth.) These things occurred so that the scripture might be fulfilled, "None of his bones shall be broken." And again another passage of scripture says, "They will look on the one whom they have pierced."

The Ugly Side of Grace

Describing grace is a challenge not easily met. However, even more difficult than explaining grace is demonstrating grace. On the way to the empty tomb and the glorious celebration of Easter, is an awkward and painful stop. It is geographically just outside the city of Jerusalem. It is a place known as the "Place of the Skull." It is tempting to hurry through this ugly place. After all, what took place here was brutal, agonizing and hard to watch. Who would want to linger long and think about the beaten and battered body of Jesus? Who would want to picture in their mind's eye the iron spikes that pierced his hands and feet? Who would want to strain to hear the echo of his cry, "It is finished"? It isn't that we are ungrateful for what he did. It's just that, well, it's an awfully gruesome sight. But to fully understand grace and the beauty of Easter, you have to look at the gruesome other side. There is no beauty without this horrific, terrible experience.

Sacrifice

For grace to be grace there has to be a sacrifice. Something has to be given which is unmerited or unearned.

The mother of a nine-year-old boy named Mark received a phone call in the middle of the afternoon. It was the teacher from her son's school.

"Mrs. Smith, something unusual happened today in your son's third grade class. Your son did something that surprised me so much that I thought you should know about it immediately."

Mark's mom began to worry.

The teacher continued, "Nothing like this has happened in all my years of teaching. This morning I was teaching a lesson on creative writing. And as I always do, I tell the story of the ant and the grasshopper: The ant works hard all summer and stores up plenty of food. But the grasshopper plays all summer and doesn't work. Then winter comes. The grasshopper begins to starve because he has no food. So he begins to beg, 'Please Mr. Ant, you have much food. Please let me eat, too.' Then I said, "Boys and girls, your job is to write the ending to the story. Your son, Mark, raised his hand. 'Teacher, may I draw a picture?' Well, yes, Mark, if you like, you may draw a picture. But first you must write the ending to the story.' As in all the years past, most of the students said the ant shared his food through the winter, and both the ant and the grasshopper lived. A few children wrote, 'No, Mr. Grasshopper. You should have worked in the summer. Now, I have just enough food for myself.' Hence, the ant lived and the grasshopper died. But your son ended the story in a way different from any other child, ever. He wrote, 'So the ant gave all of his food to the grasshopper; the grasshopper lived through the winter. But the ant died.' And the picture he drew? At the bottom of the page, Mark had drawn three crosses."

To understand grace is to understand that in order for something to be given for nothing, a price had to be paid. Mark understood that. In order for the grasshopper to live the ant had to make a sacrifice. In order for fallen man to live, Jesus, the Son, had to make a sacrifice.

Agony for Jesus

It is hard to tell where the ordeal began for Jesus. It may have been at the Passover celebration the night before when Judas went out to betray him. It may have been in the garden when he earnestly prayed for another way to accomplish his father's will. It may have been during the false accusations at the trials before Herod and Pilate. It may have been during the beatings and savage brutality that he endured. We don't know when the agony began for Jesus, but we are certain that he endured it.

He carried his own cross to the place outside the city of Jerusalem. The weight of the crossbeam may have been a hundred pounds or more. It was a painful journey to the place just outside the city: the place called "Golgotha," which means "Place of the Skull." There he was crucified with two others, criminals. That's the word they used; crucifixion. It was a particularly excruciating form of capital punishment. It's one that many civilized nations abhorred. We've read about and discussed crucifixion before, but let's take a closer look.

An article at the Christian Broadcasting Network website by Dr. C. Truman Davis reveals some important information about the history and nature of crucifixion. The article can be fully viewed here: http://www1.cbn.com/medical-view-of-the-crucifixion-of-jesus-christ. For this lesson, I'll summarize a few components.

Origin

The first known practice of crucifixion was by the Persians. Alexander and his generals brought it back to the Mediterranean world. The Romans apparently learned the practice from the Carthaginians and developed it to a higher degree of effectiveness and pain. The point of crucifixion, for the Romans, was to send a message. Dissidence would not be tolerated. It was such a gruesome punishment that the Roman citizens were generally exempt from it.

The Nails

Many of the painters and most of the sculptors of crucifixion show the nails going through the palms.

Historical accounts have established that the nails were likely driven between the small bones of the wrists and not through the palms. Nails driven through the palms would strip out between the fingers when made to support the weight of the human body. A small sign, stating the victim's crime was usually placed on a staff, carried at the front of the procession from the prison, and later nailed to the cross so that it extended above the head.

The Scourging

Preparations for the scourging were carried out when the prisoner was stripped of his clothing and his hands tied to a post above his head. It is doubtful the Romans would have made any attempt to follow the Jewish law in this matter, but the Jews had an ancient law prohibiting more than forty lashes. The Roman legionnaire steps forward with the flagrum in his hand. This is a short whip consisting of several heavy, leather thongs with two small balls of lead attached near the ends of each. The heavy whip is brought down with full force again and again across Jesus' shoulders, back, and legs. The blows are hard and continuous. The loss of blood is enormous. The scourging continues until the centurion in charge determines the one being beaten is near death.

The Long Walk

After his scourging, Jesus is forced to carry his cross. The crossbeam is tied across his shoulders and the procession of the condemned begins. Jesus, two thieves, and the execution detail of Roman soldiers headed by a centurion begins its slow journey along the Via Dolorosa. In spite of his efforts to walk erect, the weight of the heavy wooden beam, together with the shock produced by copious blood loss, is too much. He stumbles and falls. The rough wood of the beam gouges into the lacerated skin and muscles of the shoulders. He tries to rise, but human muscles have been pushed beyond their endurance. The centurion commands a stalwart North African onlooker, Simon of Cyrene, to carry the cross. Jesus follows, still bleeding, until the 650-yard journey from the fortress Antonia to Golgotha is finally completed.

Death on a Cross

Jesus is quickly thrown backward with his shoulders against the wood. The legionnaire feels for the depression at the front of the wrist. He drives a heavy, square, wrought-iron nail through the wrist and deep into the wood. Quickly, he moves to the other side and repeats the action, being careful not to pull the arms too tightly, but to allow some flexion and movement. The crossbeam is then lifted in place at the top of the stipes and the sign reading, "Jesus of Nazareth, King of the Jews," is nailed in place.

The left foot is now pressed backward against the right foot, and with both feet extended, toes down, a nail is driven through the arch of each, leaving the knees moderately flexed. Jesus is now crucified. As he slowly sags down with more weight on the nails in the wrists, excruciating pain shoots along the fingers and up the arms to explode in the brain.

Dr. Andreas Lambrianides, a general surgeon from Brisbane, Australia, wrote about crucifixion:

Crucifixion was one of the most painful, cruel, and most humiliating forms of punishment ever devised by man. The Jewish historian Josephus describes it as "the most wretched of deaths", and Seneca argues that suicide is preferable to the cruel fate of being put on the cross. Roman citizens were exempt from crucifixion except in cases of treason. Cicero called it "crudelissimum taeterrimumque supplicium" — a most cruel and disgusting punishment and he further suggested that the very word, cross, should be far removed not only from the person of a Roman citizen, but also from his thoughts, his eyes and ears, and used only in slaves, "Extremum summumque suplicium" — extreme and ultimate punishment of slaves. If the Romans regarded crucifixion with horror so did the Jews. They made no distinction between tree and cross. "Anyone who is hung on a tree is under Gods curse." Deut.21:23 they could not bring themselves to believe that the Messiah would die under a curse. (*The Cross of Christ, www.scionofzion.com/cross_of_christ.htmt*)

We can see, from the historical record, the ugliness and brutality of crucifixion.

Chaos Around the Cross

The scene around the cross at the time of the crucifixion was one of mixed emotions. Soldiers cast lots for his garments. Religious leaders derided and mocked him. Even one of the two criminals took the opportunity to ridicule Jesus. At the same time, a small group of women and the apostle John formed an island of compassion in a sea of anger and derision.

Few words are spoken as the gruesome scene unfolds. Jesus instructs John of what he wants him to do for his mother Mary. He cries out, "I thirst" and is given wine vinegar. At the end, when all is nearly complete, He exclaims, "It is finished." The word in Greek is *tetelestai* which is most often used in legal transactions to indicate that a bill had been "paid in full." Those who heard Jesus on that day knew for a certain what he was crying out. The debt that had been owed was made good. Atonement had been made for man's sins past, present and future. The centurion standing nearby pierced Jesus' side with a spear and blood and water flowed. Jesus was dead. What Paul would later write in Romans 6:23 was vividly on display: "The wages of sin is death."

Hard to Picture

Though I'm certain that I have been a bit graphic in referencing the doctors in this lesson, these sterile words on paper cannot and do not fully capture the scene as it unfolded on that day. How does one write of the agonized struggle of an innocent man willingly suffering? How does one capture in words the moment when sin past, present and future is cast upon Jesus and his father, for the first time ever, turns away? One can medically and historically describe crucifixion and yet, unless you're there, it doesn't quite resonate. The words of the Negro spiritual ring out truer than ever.

Were you there when they crucified my Lord?
Were you there when they crucified my Lord?
Oh, sometimes it causes me to tremble
(Tremble, tremble)
Were you there when they crucified my Lord?

Were you there when they nailed him to the cross?
Were you there when they nailed him to the cross?
Oh, sometimes it causes me to tremble
(Tremble, tremble)
Were you there when they nailed Him to the cross?

Were you there when they laid him in the tomb?
Were you there when they laid him in the tomb?

Oh, sometimes it causes me to tremble
(Tremble, tremble)

Were you there when they laid him in the tomb?
(in the public domain)

Grace Displayed

Grace by definition is getting that which one doesn't deserve. We celebrate God's grace at Easter, giving us life that we don't deserve. Before we go to the party, though, consider the price that was paid. The ant died so the grasshopper could get all the food. Don't forget that.

Questions

1. What is the connection between grace and sacrifice? Do you think most people connect these two? Why or why not?
2. Do you think it is hard for Christians to focus on what happened at the crucifixion? Why or why not?
3. The crucifixion was physical agony. The spiritual torture was even greater. How would you describe each of them? What does it mean to you that Jesus was willing to endure both for you?
4. Grace is giving something that is undeserved but that doesn't mean it was free. A cost had to be paid. What does that tell us about the nature of salvation? What does that tell us about God's love?

Suggested Songs or Hymns

"Alas, And Did My Savior Bleed"
"The Old Rugged Cross"
"Were You There When They Crucified My Lord"
"The Wonderful Cross"
"Lamb Of God"
"You Are My King"

Lesson 7

Grace Delivered

Lesson Objective: At the end of the lesson the participants will understand and realize that Easter means they have the opportunity to spend eternity with God in heaven.

Prayer Focus: Pray that each one in your group may carefully consider what they've heard and studied over the last six weeks. May each be drawn nearer to Jesus Christ and may those who've never yielded their lives to him do so this Easter.

Scripture Reference: John 20:1-18

Early on the first day of the week, while it was still dark, Mary Magdalene came to the tomb and saw that the stone had been removed from the tomb. So she ran and went to Simon Peter and the other disciple, the one whom Jesus loved, and said to them, "They have taken the Lord out of the tomb, and we do not know where they have laid him." Then Peter and the other disciple set out and went toward the tomb. The two were running together, but the other disciple outran Peter and reached the tomb first. He bent down to look in and saw the linen wrappings lying there, but he did not go in. Then Simon Peter came, following him, and went into the tomb. He saw the linen wrappings lying there, and the cloth that had been on Jesus' head, not lying with the linen wrappings but rolled up in a place by itself. Then the other disciple, who reached the tomb first, also went in, and he saw and believed; for as yet they did not understand the scripture, that he must rise from the dead. Then the disciples returned to their homes.

But Mary stood weeping outside the tomb. As she wept, she bent over to look into the tomb; and she saw two angels in white, sitting where the body of Jesus had been lying, one at the head and the other at the feet. They said to her, "Woman, why are you weeping?" She said to them, "They have taken away my Lord, and I do not know where they have laid him." When she had said this, she turned around and saw Jesus standing there, but she did not know that it was Jesus. Jesus said to her, "Woman, why are you weeping? Whom are you looking for?" Supposing him to be the gardener, she said to him, "Sir, if you have carried him away, tell me where you have laid him, and I will take him away." Jesus said to her, "Mary!" She turned and said to him in Hebrew, "Rabbouni!" (which means Teacher). Jesus said to her, "Do not hold on to me, because I have not yet ascended to the Father. But go to my brothers and say to them, 'I am ascending to my Father and your Father, to my God and your God.' " Mary Magdalene went and announced to the disciples, "I have seen the Lord"; and she told them that he had said these things to her.

A Time for the Unexpected

Easter is a wonderful and special time of the year. Preachers and churches look forward to Easter and make careful, thoughtful plans. It's the service in which you want everything to go smoothly. Sometimes, though, the unexpected happens.

The call to worship had just been pronounced starting Easter Sunday Morning service in an east Texas church. The choir started its processional, singing "Up From The Grave He Arose" as they marched in perfect step down the center aisle to the front of the church.

The last lady was wearing shoes with very slender heels. Without a thought for her fancy heels, she marched toward the grating that covered that hot air register in the middle of the aisle. Suddenly, the heel of one shoe sank into the hole in the register grate.

In a flash she realized her predicament. Not wishing to hold up the whole processional, without missing a step, she slipped her foot out of her shoe and continued marching down the aisle. There wasn't a hitch. The processional moved with clock-like precision. The first man after her spotted the situation and without losing a step, reached down and pulled up her shoe, but the entire grate came with it! Surprised, but still singing, the man kept on going down the aisle, holding in his hand the grate with the shoe attached.

Everything still moved like clockwork. Still in tune and still in step, the next man in line stepped into the open register and disappeared from sight. The service took on a special meaning that Sunday, for just as the choir ended with "Alleluia! Christ arose!" a voice was heard under the church shouting, "I hope all of you are out of the way 'cause I'm coming out now!"

The little girl closest to the aisle shouted, "Come on, Jesus! We'll stay out of the way."

Let Jesus Do What He Does

Easter is the celebration of grace delivered. We rejoice that sin has been covered, Satan is defeated and because Jesus lives, we can live forever. It is a great time of celebration. It is also a time, though, when it might be good for us to take the advice of the little girl and "stay out of the way" and allow Jesus to do what he needs to do.

Max Lucado, in his book *A Gentle Thunder* shares the story of a family's visit to Disney World and the remarkable thing that happened one summer day. A man and his family were inside Cinderella's castle and, as usual, it was packed with kids and parents. Suddenly, all the children rushed to one side. Had it been a boat, the castle would have tipped over. Cinderella had entered. She was the picture of beauty.

For some reason the man turned and looked toward the other side of the castle. It was now vacant except for a boy maybe seven or eight years old. His age was hard to determine because of the disfigurement of his body. Dwarfed in height, face deformed, he stood watching quietly and wistfully, holding the hand of an older brother.

It was painfully clear he wanted to be with the other children. He wanted to reach for Cinderella, too. Perhaps, though, his fear held him back. Was it fear of yet another rejection? Was it the fear of being taunted again, mocked again?

Cinderella noticed the little boy. She immediately began walking in his direction. Politely, but firmly inching through the crowd of children, she finally broke free. She walked quickly across the floor, knelt at eye level with the stunned little boy, and placed a kiss on his face.

The story Lucado recounts is a bit like what Jesus did in his grace. He reached out to us as the famous princess did to the boy. As she gave the boy a gift and showed love, Jesus offers us a gift and his love.

Jesus, though, did more than Cinderella. Cinderella gave only a kiss. When she stood to leave, she took her beauty with her. The boy was as he had been. What if Cinderella had done what Jesus did? What if she'd assumed his state? What if she had somehow given him her beauty and taken on his disfigurement? It's hard to imagine, I know, but that's what Jesus did.

Jesus, in an incredible and amazing act of grace, gave us his beauty and he bore our disfigurement to the grave. People who are surrounded by problems and heart-ache find Jesus taking all of that upon himself and giving peace in return. In the last lesson we spent some time meditating on the price paid for our sin. Today, we celebrate the beauty that is ours. Death's victim is gone. The tomb is empty. The grave stands a powerless captor. Jesus is alive!

A Sad Task

John 20 opens with the shroud of darkness still heavy upon the world. Mary Magdalene and some other women have come to the tomb. They are coming to finish the burial. The Sabbath brought about a hurried sense of getting the body off of the cross and into the tomb, so Mary and the others came, on the first day of the week, to perform one final act of kindness.

I wonder how many of us have made that same heart-wrenching journey? Hope is gone. The future is bleak. There's nothing left to do but finish it out. Every step taken on this lonesome road is a hard one, but a necessary one.

Unbelievable

However, in the middle of broken hearts and dreams, a refreshing wind blows. When they arrive at the tomb a remarkable thing has happened. The stone is rolled away. There is no body in the tomb. Mary runs to the disciples and tells them of her discovery, "They have taken away my Lord, and I do not know where they have laid him." Peter and John run to see if what the women told them is really true. It can't be, can it?

Believing the unbelievable: it's tough, isn't it? In the cynical, doubting world in which we live, taking such good news at face value and believing it is just more than a person should be expected to do. How can it be?

I saw the medical report and know the prognosis...
I heard her say that she'd never...
I've read the report and the conclusion is unmistakable...
I know what I've done and what I've thought; there's no way
I can be forgiven...
It's too late, I'm sure of it. I don't think...

Surprising Encounter

A little later, when the disciples have gone back home, Mary encounters two angels in the tomb where the body of Jesus had been. After answering their question, she turns to see a man she doesn't recognize. She thinks he is a gardener. He asks her why she's been crying and who is she looking for. She tells him about Jesus and pleads "Sir, if you have carried him away, tell me where you have laid him, and I will take him away."

Then, the man utters a one-word reply, a name actually. He says, "Mary." Maybe it was the way he said it. Maybe at that moment the veil of darkness was lifted. Maybe the shadow gave way to the light. Whatever the cause, it was at that moment that Mary realized that this man was no gardener. He was her Lord, himself. Jesus was alive. She is overcome and falls at his feet. Jesus tells her not to hold on to him, but to go and tell his brothers that he had risen.

Jesus is alive! The bridge that connected God and humanity is restored. God's grace has been delivered.

Challenges Ahead

Challenges emerge from the empty tomb. The first of these is will you accept this gift of grace? Lent is not about just giving up something in order to be a better person. It's recognizing what Jesus did in giving us the opportunity for life. We give up something at Lent because we want to identify with Jesus. There is nothing more important that you could do for Lent than to give yourself to Jesus.

A second challenge also streams from the empty tomb. For those who already follow Jesus, will you help others come to know him? Will you take the advice of the little girl at the beginning of this lesson and get out of the way, so that people will see the Lord?

A boy came to church with his grandmother fairly regularly. In this church, the pulpit stood in front of a painting of Jesus. The church's regular preacher was a humble man who happened to be of small stature. On this particular Sunday, a guest preacher was speaking. He was a loud, boisterous speaker and a rather large man. The boy noticed the difference right away.

He whispered to his grandmother, "Hey Grandma, who is this new guy that's blocking our view of Jesus?"

Let Jesus shine forth this Easter. Resolve that others see him in your words and actions.

God has given us a wonderful gift in his son Jesus Christ. Grace. Is there any word more beautiful? Is any word more powerful? When problems and trouble confront you on every side, remember, you're surrounded by grace.

Questions
1. The Cinderella story in this lesson is a powerful one. Cinderella did a nice thing for the boy, but Jesus did even more. He took our sinful self to give us his spotless self. What does that tell us about the nature of grace?
2. Sometimes it can be really dark before the sunrise. That's true in a lot of ways. What does the resurrection of Jesus tell us about the hard things that come our way?
3. What does it mean to give yourself to Jesus? What does that look like in everyday life?
4. How do we get in the way of people seeing Jesus? What can we do about it?

Suggested Songs or Hymns
"Up From The Grave He Arose"
"He Lives"
"I Will Rise"
"My Redeemer Lives"
"Glorious Day"
"Amazing Grace"